The Nez Perce

Sharlene and Ted Nelson

WattsLIBRARY™

Franklin Watts
A Division of Scholastic Inc.
New York • Toronto • London • Auckland • Sydney
Mexico City • New Delhi • Hong Kong
Danbury, Connecticut

To all the Nez Perce, especially those who helped us,
and Naomi Martin Kulp, whose ancestors traveled the Oregon Trail.

Note to readers: Definitions for words in **bold** can be found in the Glossary at the back of this book.

Photographs © 2003: Art Resource, NY/Smithsonian American Art Museum, Washington, DC: 18; Clymer Museum of Art, courtesy of Mrs. John Clymer: 11 (Pride of the Nez Perce, by John F. Clymer), 35 (Old Nez Perce Trail, by John F. Clymer); David Jensen: 10, 12, 36, 38; Idaho State Historical Society/E. Jane Gay: 41; Karen Bryant: 14; Library of Congress: 8; Montana Historical Society, Helena: 24 (Maud Davis Baker), 43 (Tolman); National Park Service, Nez Perce National Historical Park: 19 left (NEPE-HI-0097), 19 right (NEPE-HI-0156), 26 (NEPE-HI-1144), 27 (NEPE-HI-1144), 9 (NEPE-HI-1786), 50 (NEPE #8760); Nativestock.com/Marilyn "Angel" Wynn: 3 right, 44, 45, 47, 48; Penrose Memorial Library/Northwest and Whitman College Archives: 40; Scotts Bluff National Monument: 21; Smithsonian Institution, Washington, DC: 3 left, 30 (Jay F. Haynes), 34 (William Henry Jackson); The Greenwich Workshop, Inc./Howard Terpning: 37; University of Washington Libraries/E.W. Moore/MSCUA: 32 (NA 878); Washington State Historical Society, Tacoma: 23 (Sohon #36), 29 (Sohon #53).

Cover illustration by Gary Overacre, based on a photograph from the Smithsonian Institution by Jay F. Haynes.

Map by XNR Productions Inc.

Library of Congress Cataloging-in-Publication Data

Nelson, Sharlene P.
    The Nez Perce / by Sharlene and Ted Nelson
        p. cm—(Watts library)
    Includes bibliographical references and index.
    Contents: Reminders of the past—the early ways—Times of change—Broken promises—An unwanted war—More promises broken—A people renewed.
    ISBN 0-531-12169-0 (lib. bdg.)   0-531-16216-8 (pbk.)
    1. Nez Perce Indians—Juvenile literature. [1. Nez Perce Indians. 2. Indians of North America—Northwest, Pacific.] I. Nelson, Ted W. II. Title. III. Series.
E99.N5N45 2003
979.5004'9741—dc21

                                                  2003000959

Contents

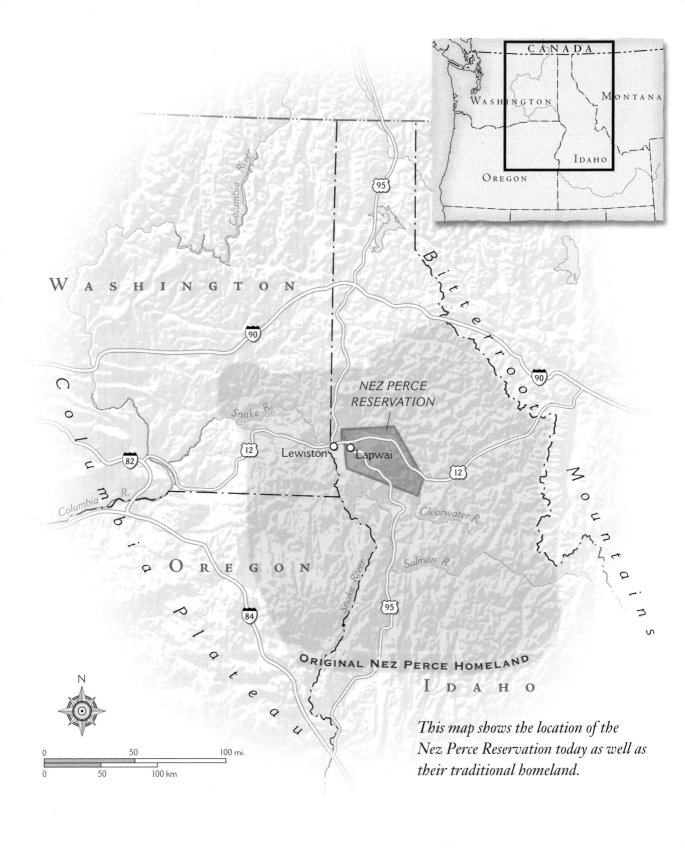

This map shows the location of the Nez Perce Reservation today as well as their traditional homeland.

Chapter One

The Early Ways

The ancestors of the modern Nez Perce people roamed freely over lands of forested mountains, deep canyons, valleys, prairies, and grass-covered hills. The Snake River cuts through these lands on the eastern part of the Columbia Plateau in what is today part of north central Idaho, southeastern Washington, and northeastern Oregon. The Bitterroot Mountains bounded their lands on the east. To the west, their lands extended to the plains of the plateau. From the Bitterroots, the Clearwater and Salmon Rivers flow into the Snake. The original homeland of the Nez Perce was larger than the states of New Hampshire and Vermont combined. Stone tools have been found that indicate people have lived in the region for nearly eleven thousand years.

A Nez Perce legend says that long ago, all the earth's people were killed by a monster. Coyote killed the monster and tore him to pieces. He threw pieces of the monster to different parts of the land, which caused different people to spring up. Finally, he squeezed the blood from the monster's heart. The blood became the Nez Perce people.

The Nez Perce believed they were spiritually related to the land and all of nature. The earth was their mother, who nourished them. The trees, mountains, rivers, and the plants and animals that provided their food were a part of the Nez Perce family. Uniting all these together was a Great Spirit called the

Creator. Before and after meals and ceremonies, they sang prayers of gratitude to the Creator.

Villages, Bands, and Chiefs

The Nez Perce's permanent homes were clustered in villages scattered along the Snake, Salmon, and Clearwater Rivers, and their **tributaries**. The residents of each village were usually related to each other. There were mothers, fathers, grandparents, children, aunts, uncles, nieces, nephews, and cousins.

The earliest Nez Perce lived in dwellings that were pits dug into the ground and covered with log and sod roofs. Later, **reed** mats tied to poles formed the walls and roofs above the shallow pits. In villages where few people lived, the dwellings were small and circular. In villages of two hundred or more people, several families lived together in A-shaped lodges up to 150 feet (46 meters) long. Cooking fires glowed in trenches in the center of the dwellings. For cleansing body and mind, small, sod-covered sweat houses stood nearby.

The members of each village formed a **band** with a chief, or headman, as their leader. The chief looked after the band's well-being, settled disputes, and gave advice on important matters. Chiefs usually inherited their title from their fathers. Most chiefs had proven themselves skilled in battle against their enemies.

To make decisions affecting the entire tribe, each band's chief, several warriors, and important **elders** traveled long distances on foot or by dugout canoe to meet in a tribal council.

The Sweat House Tradition

In a sweat house, water was poured on fire-heated rocks to make steam. When covered with sweat, bathers plunged into a cold stream.

The Nez Perce carved canoes from pine logs.

However, individual bands did not have to abide by the decisions made at the council. Each band could do as it pleased.

Nez Perce Seasons

The Nez Perce spent winters in permanent villages in the lower valleys, where snows were seldom deep. Inside the fire-lit dwellings, children began to learn the tribe's ways. Women wove baskets and made animal-skin clothes, moccasins, and bearskin robes. Men prepared their spears and arrows for fishing and hunting. They made strong bows with strips cut from the horns of mountain sheep.

Spears were used to catch salmon.

With the arrival of spring, each band began collecting enough food to sustain its members through the next winter. Men and boys caught salmon and other fish and eels with spears and nets or in traps made of brush and poles. From spring through fall, people in each village caught thousands of salmon. Women roasted the fish over fires to be eaten fresh. More fish were dried in the sun or smoked for storage.

As the winter snows melted, the bands began leaving their permanent villages to hunt and to gather roots and berries in the higher country. The reed mats from the permanent dwellings were taken along for temporary shelter. The women

Salmon Cycles

Salmon are born in rivers and streams and then swim to the ocean. After several years, they return to the rivers and streams to deposit and fertilize their eggs.

The blue-flowered camas plants were a source of food for the Nez Perce.

carried digging sticks with sharp points and stone or bone handles. In favorite places, they dug for the roots of the **kouse**, which is a wild parsley plant. The roots were boiled or steamed into a mush that was patted into biscuitlike cakes to be eaten fresh or stored.

In midsummer, the villagers sought the roots of the **camas** plant, which is a type of lily. Many bands gathered on prairies where the camas grew. Men and boys hunted or played games while women and girls dug the roots. The roots were cooked and pounded into cakes for storage. From summer through fall, huckleberries, blackberries, and wild strawberries were picked by the basketful. The berries were pressed into cakes and stored. The women also gathered leaves, bark, and fruit from other plants. The Nez Perce used these to heal wounds and cure common **ailments**, such as coughs and colds.

The men and boys had favorite places to hunt for deer, elk, mountain sheep, and bear. Armed with spears, bows, and arrows, and disguised with animal skins from previous kills, the hunters stalked their prey. On other hunts, they formed long lines to encircle the animals. To catch smaller animals, such as rabbits and wolves, traps were set. Villagers feasted on the fresh, cooked meat or dried it for storage.

The Horse and the Buffalo

The ways of the Nez Perce changed when they obtained horses in the early 1700s. Before acquiring horses, dogs were used to carry their belongings. At first, the horses, like the dogs, were used to carry heavy loads. Gradually, the Nez Perce became experts at riding. Hunting became easier, warriors rode into battle, and bands rode long distances to meet in council or to trade with other tribes.

The lives of the Nez Perce changed after they acquired horses.

The Arrival of the Horse

Spanish explorers introduced horses from Europe to the American Southwest in the 1500s.

Through capture or trade, American Indians brought the horses north.

This photograph shows a traditional tepee.

The Nez Perce homeland was ideal for raising horses. In winter, the horses grazed in the lower valleys. In summer, mountain meadows provided them with lush grass to eat. The Nez Perce learned to **breed** horses for strength and endurance. Each band had hundreds of well-bred horses that became prized items of trade among all the people the Nez Perce encountered.

Many Nez Perce bands began riding east across the Rocky Mountains to hunt buffalo on the **Great Plains**. The bands camped and hunted with their friends, the Crow Indians.

They adopted the elaborately decorated clothes and feathered headdresses worn by the Plains Indians. The Plains **tepee** became their preferred dwelling. It was made of buffalo skin stretched over a framework of poles.

Growing Up Nez Perce

Infants were placed in **cradleboards**, which are leather pouches with straps. The straps enabled mothers to carry infants on their backs. Boys played with toy bows. Girls played with toy digging sticks. By the age of six, boys helped with fishing and hunting, while girls helped with gathering roots and berries. Grandfathers taught boys to ride, fish, and hunt. To ensure that a boy would become a good provider, an expert fisher or hunter ate the first animal the boy killed. Grandmothers taught girls to gather roots and berries. To ensure their future success, an expert gatherer ate the first roots collected by a girl.

Because the Nez Perce had no written language, elders told children the tribe's legends. They also taught them the sacred songs and dances. This assured that the tribe's traditions would be passed on from generation to generation.

Each child was taught to find his or her *Wyakin*, a mystical spirit guide found in the child's natural surroundings. This spiritlike guardian would guide and protect the child during his or her adult life. To find their *Wyakin*, each boy and girl between the age of nine and fifteen was sent on a vision quest.

The Vision Quest

Alone and without food, a young Nez Perce sat on a ridge or a mound of rocks. In deep, almost dreamlike thought, the child hoped that his or her *Wyakin* would appear. After many hours, and sometimes days, the child might find his or her *Wyakin*. If the spirit came, it could be in the form of lightning across a darkened sky, in the howl of a wolf, as an eagle soaring, or in any number of natural ways.

Explorers Lewis and Clark, shown here with Sacagawea, a Shoshone Indian, reached the Nez Perce homeland in 1805.

Chapter Two

Times of Change

In September of 1805, Captains Meriwether Lewis and William Clark became the first white people to reach the Nez Perce homeland. They, with twenty-nine men and a Shoshone Indian woman carrying her seven-month-old baby, arrived on horses. The captains had been sent west by President Thomas Jefferson in the hope of finding a water route to the Pacific Ocean. They had traveled more than 3,000 miles (4,800 kilometers) from near St. Louis on the banks of the Mississippi River. They still had to travel 500 miles (800 km) to reach the Pacific.

The explorers had struggled over the Bitterroot Mountains in deep snow. They had found no elk or deer for food and were starving. Hearing of their arrival, an elderly Nez Perce woman named Watkuweis told the others to welcome the strangers.

Lewis and Clark were also welcomed because the Nez Perce wanted to establish trade for guns with white people. Some tribes on the plains carried guns obtained from Canadian traders. The Nez Perce wanted them for hunting and defense.

The Nez Perce gave the explorers food and shelter and helped them make dugout canoes to complete their westward journey. They drew a map on elk skin that showed the river route to the Pacific Ocean. Two Nez Perce accompanied Lewis and Clark for a time to ensure that the tribes to the west would welcome them.

In 1806, Lewis and Clark returned from the Pacific Ocean. They stayed with the Nez Perce for several weeks as they waited for snows to melt in the Bitterroots. Patrick Gass, an expedition member, wrote that the Nez Perce were "the most friendly, honest, and ingenious" of all the tribes they met.

The Fur Trappers

Six years later, fur trappers began coming to the Nez Perce homeland. They were searching for beaver. Beaver fur was used to make top hats worn by men in the eastern United States and Europe. For the next thirty years, trappers roamed the West in search of the prized fur.

The trappers were tough men who waded in icy streams to set their traps. They worked for Canadian, British, and American fur-trading companies. The companies provided the trappers with guns, ammunition, bright-colored cloth, beads, and thimbles. The trappers traded these goods with American Indians for food, horses, and help in finding beaver. The goods the Nez Perce received made them more important trading partners with other tribes.

From the trappers, the Nez Perce learned about Christianity and the Bible. They thought the trappers' religious beliefs were the source of the trappers' wealth and skill. With no written language of their own, they also marveled at the trappers' ability to make paper "talk."

In 1825, a British fur-trading company sent two boys from neighboring tribes to a Christian school in Canada. They were

"Talking Paper"

The Nez Perce called messages and letters scrawled on paper with pen and ink "talking paper."

Rabbit Skin Leggings was among the four Nez Perce who traveled to St. Louis.

sons of chiefs. When they returned four years later, they could write and speak English and read the Bible. The Nez Perce heard about the boys and wanted to learn the same skills to increase their power. In 1831, four Nez Perce traveled to St. Louis with a group of American fur traders. They met with William Clark, whom they had befriended years before. They told Clark they wanted Christian teachers to teach them about the Bible, which they called the "white man's book from Heaven."

The Missionaries

Word of the Nez Perce journey to St. Louis spread to Christian **missionaries** in the East. In 1836, the Presbyterian Henry H. Spalding and his wife Eliza, and Dr. Marcus Whitman and his wife Narcissa traveled west along the fur trappers' trails. The Whitmans established a mission among the Cayuse, a tribe whose lands neighbored the Nez Perce to the

Welcoming the Missionaries' Wives

The missionaries' wives were the first white women seen by the Nez Perce. The Nez Perce women greeted them with kisses, because trappers had said that was the way white women greeted each other.

west. The Spaldings established their mission at the Nez Perce village of Lapwai on the Clearwater River.

The Spaldings built a school where Eliza began teaching the Nez Perce to read and write. Reverend Spalding led religious services on Sundays and showed the Nez Perce how to plant orchards and crops of grain. They built a **gristmill** to make flour and a sawmill to make lumber.

Many of the Nez Perce adopted the Christian faith, including two important chiefs. One was Chief Hallalhotsoot, whose band lived east of Lapwai on the Clearwater River. The

Missionaries Henry Spalding (left) and Marcus Whitman (right), came west to teach Christianity.

The Oregon Trail

The Oregon Trail stretched from Independence, Missouri, to Oregon's Columbia River. Traveling the more than 2,000-mile (3,200-km)-long trail took about five months.

Spaldings called this chief, Lawyer. The other was Chief Tuekakas of the Wallowa band, whom the Spaldings called Joseph. However, not all the Nez Perce adopted the missionaries' teachings. Spalding had a quick temper and was often abusive. Many men considered working in the fields to be women's work. They also believed the ground was sacred and not to be dug with hoes or plows. They didn't want to live in one place and be farmers. They wanted to hunt buffalo.

Settlers and Strife

While the missionaries worked among their followers, people in the East were hearing of free and fertile lands in the West. It was a place to start a new life. In 1841, wagon trains began traveling west along the Oregon Trail. By 1847, more than ten thousand **emigrants** had traveled the trail. Most of them crossed the Columbia Plateau on their way to Oregon's Willamette Valley.

The trail crossed the lands of the Cayuse in mountains south of the Whitman's mission. The emigrants brought diseases to the region, and many Cayuse became sick with measles. Dr. Whitman tried to help them, but many died. To avenge the deaths, a small group of Cayuse warriors attacked the mission. Dr. Whitman, Narcissa, and twelve others were killed in what became known as the "Whitman Massacre." The Whitman mission was abandoned, and the Spaldings left their mission.

Soldiers came from the Willamette Valley to fight the

Cayuse and capture the murderers. Men on both sides were killed in battle. Some of the Cayuse escaped, and the soldiers followed the fugitives to Lapwai. The Christian Nez Perce did not want to be drawn into battle. Joseph said, "I do not want my children engaged in this war . . . ." Lawyer told his followers that the soldiers had the right to capture the murderers. Their refusal to fight prevented a larger war, and the fugitives were captured.

Thousands of emigrants came west along the Oregon Trail.

Treaties and Turmoil

In 1853, Washington became a United States territory. Its first governor, Issac Stevens, set out to make **treaties** with the tribes living in the territory. Under these agreements, the tribes would give up land to make room for settlers. In May of 1855, Stevens and other officials met with several tribes of the Columbia Plateau at a place not far from the old Whitman mission. The tribes included the Nez Perce, Cayuse, Umatilla, and Yakima.

More than five thousand American Indians went to the meeting. There were chiefs, elders, warriors, and their families. One observer wrote that when the Nez Perce arrived, "a thousand warriors mounted on fine horses" galloped onto the meeting ground. He described them as "decked with plumes and feathers and trinkets fluttering in the sunshine."

Stevens promised that the United States government would build schools, supply clothing and farming tools, and pay the tribes for the lands they gave up. He pointed at maps showing the lands where each tribe would be allowed to live. He called these areas **reservations**. Stevens said white people would not be allowed on the reservations unless they had the tribes' permission. The meeting lasted nearly two weeks as the talk was translated back and forth between English and the languages of the tribes.

In June of 1855, the chiefs signed treaty agreements with Stevens. Some tribes gave up all of their lands and agreed to move to reservations shared with other tribes. The Nez Perce gave up much of their homeland, but retained the lands that were most important to them for hunting and gathering roots.

Then, gold was discovered on the Columbia Plateau. Miners began crossing reservation lands near the Columbia River.

Washington Territory

Washington Territory included the lands that are now the states of Washington, Idaho, and parts of Montana and Wyoming.

The tribes felt betrayed. Angry warriors killed some miners. U.S. soldiers came to avenge the killings. Battles erupted and turned into a war that lasted until 1858. Hundreds of soldiers fought against warriors from five tribes. Again, influenced by their Christian chiefs, the Nez Perce were not drawn into the war. Nez Perce warriors served as scouts for the United States Army and helped ferry soldiers and their horses across the Snake River.

Nez Perce warriors paraded for Governor Stevens and other officials as treaty negotiations began.

Miners panned for gold on the Nez Perce Reservation.

Chapter Three

Broken Promises

Settlement on the Columbia Plateau was banned during the war. When the war ended in 1858, settlers began moving onto the lands outside the reservations. No white people ventured near the remote Nez Perce Reservation until February of 1860. Then, two miners with picks, shovels, and gold pans came up a tributary of the Clearwater River in search of gold.

One of the miners reported finding gold in "every place they tried." A few months later, he returned with ten more prospectors. They made a rich gold strike, and word of the discovery spread throughout the West.

Overpowered by Gold

In the spring of 1861, thousands of miners rushed onto the Nez Perce Reservation in search of gold. A paddle wheel steamboat began making regular trips up the Snake River from the Columbia River. The boat brought miners, merchants, and their supplies. Lawyer made an agreement allowing the boats to land at the mouth of the Clearwater River on reservation lands. Almost overnight, a town of twelve hundred people sprang up. There were houses, stores, hotels, shops, and saloons. The town was named Lewiston, and in 1863, it became the first capital of the new territory of Idaho.

As miners fanned out across the reservation east of the Snake River, many Nez Perce were caught up in the gold rush. Some prospered by selling horses, cattle, and produce to the miners. Others became laborers who loaded pack

Panning for Gold

Miners sloshed water and river sediment in shallow pans to wash away sand and gravel, leaving the heavier gold in the bottom of the pan.

Steamboats brought miners and settlers to the Nez Perce Reservation.

mules and wagons. For some Nez Perce, their way of life gave
way to the often rowdy life of the miners.

More Homeland Taken

Under the treaty of 1855, the miners were not supposed to be on the reservation without the Nez Perce's permission. But the miners were there, and more were coming. In May of 1863, Calvin Hale, a representative of the U.S. government, met with the Nez Perce to make a new treaty to provide more land for settlement.

Hale said the government wanted all the Nez Perce to live on a small reservation around Lapwai. He said the government would pay for the lands that were to be taken. The chiefs and bands who would lose their lands were unwilling to discuss a new treaty. They left the meeting and returned to their villages, intent on keeping the lands promised to them in 1855.

With the few chiefs that remained, Hale concluded the treaty for a new reservation. The treaty took nearly 7,000,000 acres (2,832,000 hectares) from the reservation agreed to in 1855. The Nez Perce retained only 757,000 acres (306,342 ha).

A Tribe Divided

Only Lawyer and the chiefs who supported him signed the 1863 treaty. They were already living on the lands within the smaller reservation. They would have to give up nothing. These bands became known as the treaty bands.

The bands that did not sign the treaty became known as the nontreaty bands. Because they did not sign the treaty, they believed they would be allowed to keep the lands reserved for them in 1855. Among these were Chief White Bird's Salmon River band and Joseph's Wallowa band.

Lawyer
Hal-hal-tlos Tsot

Many members of the nontreaty bands, including Joseph, abandoned their Christian faith. The benefits they had sought by accepting the church had only turned to trouble with the flood of miners and settlers that followed the missionaries. They returned to their early beliefs in their Creator and their reverence for Mother Earth seemed better now.

Young Joseph became chief of the Wallowa band when his father died.

Chapter Four

An Unwanted War

Little changed for the nontreaty bands immediately after 1863. Those bands living east of the Snake River remained on their lands and endured the presence of miners and settlers. Joseph's band remained in Oregon's Wallowa Valley, west of the Snake River, where no gold was found. In August of 1871, Old Joseph died. His son, also named Joseph, became the band's chief. As the old chief lay dying, he said, "My son, my body

returns to my mother earth . . . . Never sell the bones of your father and mother."

The year young Joseph became chief, settlers started moving into the Wallowa Valley. Disputes arose over who could use the grasslands to graze their livestock. Each side accused the other of stealing horses and cattle. To keep the peace, Joseph visited the settlers' cabins and made friends with them and their children. Joseph and his trusted brother Ollokot, the leader of the band's warriors, told their young men not to make trouble with the settlers.

Ollokot, Chief Joseph's brother, became leader of the Wallowa band's warriors.

Chief Joseph: The Patriot Chief

Chief Joseph was thirty-one years old when he became chief of the Wallowa band after the death of his father. Unlike most Nez Perce chiefs, Joseph had not fought as a warrior or hunted buffalo. His strengths were in his kindness and patience, and his loyalty to his beliefs and his people. Later, as a chief in a war he did not want, his greatest commitment was to the care of the women and children, the elderly, the sick and the wounded. Through newspaper reports of the war's progress, Joseph became the symbol of a people fighting for their beliefs against overwhelming odds.

Threats to Peace

Despite efforts toward peace, disputes on both sides of the Snake River became worse. In 1876, General Oliver O. Howard, speaking for the United States government, told the nontreaty bands that they would have to move. They were ordered to sell their lands and go to the reservation established in the 1863 treaty. The nontreaty bands reminded Howard that they had not agreed to that treaty. Recalling his father's words, Chief Joseph told Howard that his lands were "too sacred to be valued by or sold for silver or gold."

In May of 1877, Howard gave the nontreaty bands thirty days to move to Lapwai. He told Joseph that if there were any delay, "soldiers will be there to drive you on the reservation." Joseph was saddened. He could not sell the lands of his father, yet he did not want war. Reluctantly, he told his band of nearly two hundred people to collect their belongings and gather their horses and cattle. Then, Joseph and Ollokot led the band out of the Wallowa Valley and across the Snake River toward Lapwai.

Near Lapwai, Joseph's band joined other nontreaty bands, including the band of Chief White Bird. The bands gathered to enjoy a few days of freedom before going to the reservation. One morning, three of White Bird's angry warriors rode off to avenge the wrongs they had suffered at the hands of the intruders. Several settlers were killed. Alarmed, the bands began to move away from Lapwai. Joseph and Ollokot argued for going peacefully to the reservation, but it was too late.

General Oliver O. Howard

General Howard, a Civil War veteran, helped establish Howard University for freed slaves in Washington, D.C. Today, the college enrolls a large number of African-American students.

33

Chief Looking Glass joined in the war after soldiers attacked his village.

Alerted by frightened settlers, General Howard sent his troops to fight against the bands. In June, the Nez Perce defeated Howard's soldiers at the Battle of White Bird Canyon. Howard called in more troops. After soldiers attacked Chief Looking Glass's village, he and his people joined the nontreaty bands. In July, Howard defeated the Nez Perce at the Battle of the Clearwater. Despite the defeat, the Nez Perce avoided capture.

Escape to the Plains

The bands decided to escape to the Great Plains. They thought their buffalo-hunting friends, the Crow, would help them. With Howard's troops in pursuit, the Nez Perce headed east through the Lolo Pass along the Lolo Trail. For days, two hundred men, more than five hundred women and children, and two thousand horses struggled on the steep, rocky trail.

On August 7, 1877, the Nez Perce reached Montana's Big Hole River. Confident they had escaped Howard's troops, the Nez Perce stopped to rest. For the first time in weeks, nighttime guards were not posted. The Nez Perce were unaware that troops from forts in Montana were nearing their camp.

34

At dawn on August 9, soldiers attacked the sleeping Nez Perce. Rifle and canon fire ripped through the tepees. The warriors fought back. Chief Joseph helped gather the horses and assisted the women and children in collecting their belongings. Those who had been killed were hastily buried, and the wounded cared for. Ollokot, Chief Looking Glass, and their warriors held the soldiers back while Joseph and the families fled.

The Battle of the Big Hole dealt a severe blow to the Nez Perce. Twelve warriors had been killed. More than sixty women and children were dead, and many were wounded. Desperate for peace but unwilling to give up, they traveled on.

The Nez Perce moved east through Yellowstone National Park, where they captured, and then released several frightened tourists. From the park, the bands turned north toward

The Nez Perce crossed over Lolo Pass on the way to the Plains.

The Lolo Trail

The Lolo Trail, which crosses the Bitterroot Mountains, was a route the Nez Perce took to the Plains and was used by Lewis and Clark.

A cannon such as this was used against the Nez Perce at the Battle of Big Hole.

the Plains. Each time the soldiers came close enough to fight, the Nez Perce warriors turned them back. When they reached the Plains, the Nez Perce found that the Crow had turned against them to fight with the army. Now, their only chance for escape was to reach Canada.

"Fight No More Forever"

Yellowstone National Park

The park, established in 1872, is the nation's oldest national park.

On September 28, 1877, the Nez Perce reached Montana's Bear Paw Mountains, only 40 miles (64 km) from Canada. Again, thinking that Howard's troops were far behind, they stopped to rest. But troops under Colonel Nelson B. Miles were fast approaching. On September 30, Miles's troops made two fierce charges against the Nez Perce. Many soldiers and Nez Perce were killed, including Ollokot and Chief Looking

Glass. Unable to defeat the Nez Perce, Miles's soldiers surrounded the weary bands to await the arrival of General Howard's troops four days later.

The Nez Perce had traveled 1,150 miles (1,840 km) and fought against nearly two thousand soldiers. Nearly one hundred Nez Perce had been killed and many others wounded. Some, including Chief White Bird, managed to break through the lines to reach Canada. The army's losses totaled more than two hundred killed and wounded.

On October 5, 1877, with bitter winds blowing the first snows of winter, Chief Joseph rode out to surrender. He told Colonel Miles and General Howard, "From where the sun now stands, I will fight no more forever."

Chief Joseph rode out to surrender to end the war of 1877.

The Nez Perce found Oklahoma a difficult place to live and dreamed of returning to their homeland.

Chapter Five

More Promises Broken

When the Nez Perce bands surrendered in 1877, they were told that they could return to Idaho. Instead, the government sent them to Kansas and then to Oklahoma. Many became sick and died in the hot and humid climate. Joseph began a campaign for the return of his people to their homeland. In 1879, he traveled to

Though this newspaper illustration depicts a peaceful scene, the Nez Perce suffered in captivity and many people died.

Washington, D.C., to meet with President Rutherford B. Hayes. Nelson Miles, by then a general, befriended Joseph and helped him.

In 1885, the Nez Perce were allowed to leave Oklahoma. Many returned to the reservation in Idaho. Because of ill feelings with other Nez Perce bands over the war, Chief Joseph and his band were sent to Nespelem, Washington, on the Colville Indian Reservation. Two years later, the United States Congress passed the General Allotment Act. Under the act, each western Indian would receive an **allotment** of land. Those who received an allotment would become a United States citizen. This act brought more change for the Nez Perce.

Lands Given, Lands Taken

The Nez Perce were among the first tribes affected by the act. Each tribal member would be given an allotment of land of up to 160 acres (65 ha) within the Nez Perce Reservation. Lands not allotted would be sold to settlers and the money given to tribal members. Congress thought that when the Nez Perce and other American Indians became landowners, they would quickly become a part of white society. Congress also knew the act would make more land available to settlers.

In 1889, Alice Fletcher and a surveyor came to the reservation to enforce the act. At first, Fletcher encountered resistance. Many Nez Perce did not trust the government, and the Nez Perce had always shared their lands with each other. The

Alice Fletcher (far left) explained land allotments to a gathering of Nez Perce.

idea of individual land ownership was foreign to them. But Fletcher, called the "Measuring Woman" by the Nez Perce, worked honestly and patiently. The surveyor marked the reservation boundary and pounded stakes into the ground to mark each allotment.

Gradually, Fletcher convinced the Nez Perce to accept their allotments. To simplify government record keeping, each person was required to adopt an American name in place of his or her sacred Nez Perce name. By 1892, Fletcher had measured nearly two thousand allotments. The remaining lands, almost 500,000 acres (202,340 ha) of the 757,000-acre (306,343 ha) reservation, were sold to settlers.

No Return for Joseph

Chief Joseph would not accept an allotment on the reservation. He still hoped to return with his people to the Wallowa Valley. In 1897 and 1903, Joseph traveled to Washington, D.C., to ask to be allowed to return to his homeland. His requests were denied. Joseph visited the Wallowa Valley in 1903 and never returned.

Joseph became a national celebrity. He rode in a New York City parade with General Howard at his side and appeared in shows that depicted American Indian life. He lectured at colleges and universities to help historians understand the events of 1877. He became a friend to American Indian and white children.

Chief Joseph died in 1904. He was sixty-four years old. His doctor said he died of a broken heart.

A Tribe in Decline

The General Allotment Act did not help make the Nez Perce a part of white society. The individual allotments were too small to produce profits from farming or cattle raising. Many Nez Perce rented their allotments to settlers and moved away. Others stayed to work in sawmills, in logging, or in the small towns that sprang up within the reservation.

In the early 1900s, many Nez Perce were living in poverty and suffering from diseases. A tribe that had numbered more than six thousand people when Lewis and Clark encountered them had declined to about two thousand. A 1911 government report stated, "It will only be a few generations before the tribe is extinct."

Unable to return to the Wallowa Valley, Chief Joseph remained at Nespelem, Washington, until he died in 1904.

43

Many of the Nez Perce celebrate their culture by participating in events, such as the Wallowa Valley Friendship Feast and Powwow shown here.

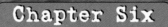

Chapter Six

A People Renewed

Despite the prediction of their extinction, the Nez Perce have renewed their lives and culture. Many are again appearing in feathered headdresses, beaded clothes, and moccasins at **powwows**, pageants, and festivals. Some gather for Friendship Feasts, where they share food with visitors and dance to traditional drum rhythms and chant sacred songs.

The recovery of the Nez Perce did not come easily. For many years the children were punished for speaking Nez Perce in school. They stopped listening to the elders who told the tribe's legends, and their language was almost lost. Girls did not learn the ancient skills of weaving and beadwork. As they grew older, many young people left to work in cities, serve in the armed forces, and attend college. While they were gone, many elders died, and traditions died with them.

A Government of Their Own

The Nez Perce organized their first government, the "Home and Farm Association," in 1923. Its intent was to improve conditions on the reservation. In 1948, the Nez Perce of the Nez Perce Indian Reservation adopted a new constitution and by-laws. Descendants of Chief Joseph and his band live under a similar tribal government among the Confederated Tribes of the Colville Indian Reservation in Washington. Others live among the Confederated Tribes of the Umatilla Indian Reservation in Oregon.

At Lapwai, a nine-member Nez Perce Tribal Executive Committee governs thirty-two hundred tribal members. Their staff manages the reservation's business and the tribe's social and natural resources. Tribal archaeologists help discover and preserve ancient Nez Perce sites. Foresters oversee timber harvesting and wildlife management on tribal lands. Fish biologists raise salmon in hatcheries on Snake River tributaries. The hatchery fish help offset the loss of the once great natural salmon runs. These runs declined because of the loss of habitat and the construction of dams on the Columbia and Snake Rivers.

The tribe operates a store, an outpatient clinic, and a school. Many of the doctors, nurses, and teachers are Nez Perce. After living away from the reservation, these professionals have returned to assist their tribe. Trained law-enforcement officers on the reservation are Nez Perce. Nez Perce men and women own businesses. Several Nez Perce living in Lapwai provide a variety of services from building construction to an arts council. One family business continues the tradition of raising Appaloosa horses, a horse favored by the early Nez Perce.

Smoke shops, trading posts selling Nez Perce crafts, and consulting firms are located in nearby and distant cities. Like many American Indian tribes, the Nez Perce operate casinos. They are both located in Idaho, one at Kamiah, and one near Lewiston.

This photograph shows some traditional Nez Perce crafts.

Restoring Early Ways

A revival of the Nez Perce language helped restore the tribe's traditions. In the 1960s, Haruo Aoki, a Japanese-American scholar, came to listen to the few elders who still spoke Nez Perce. From his studies, Aoki wrote a Nez Perce dictionary, texts, and a grammar book. Adults and children are now learning the language, which is taught at the tribal school.

Nez Perce youths are again listening to their elders and learning to appreciate the value of being Nez Perce. Many children are given Nez Perce names in addition to their

Today, many Nez Perce children are learning the ways of their ancestors.

American names. Some children go on vision quests. Some are learning to ride and care for horses as their ancestors did. The Nez Perce Young Horsemen Project teaches these skills to youths fourteen to twenty-one years old.

In Oregon's Wallowa Valley, the Wallowa Band Nez Perce are developing a historical site with interpretive trails, a dance arbor, and a cultural center. Each July, visitors and Nez Perce from western states gather in the valley. They come to enjoy Chief Joseph Days and Tamkaliks Celebration with parades, Friendship Feasts, and ceremonial dancing.

Artifacts Reclaimed

In 1996, Nez Perce efforts toward restoring their culture gained national attention. The tribe held a fund-raising campaign to purchase a collection of 150-year-old Nez Perce **artifacts** that belonged to the Ohio historical society. The collection contained the oldest known examples of Nez Perce artistry. Among the artifacts was a woman's elk-hide dress decorated with elk teeth and beads, a man's elk-hide shirt, and a woman's saddle. Tribal Chairman Samuel N. Penney called them "dynamic reflections of who we, the Nez Perce are as a people."

Missionary Henry Spalding bought the artifacts in the 1840s with trade goods worth $57.90 and sent them to a friend living in Ohio. Eventually, the historical society acquired them. In 1996, they were worth $608,100.

The tribe was given six months to raise more than $600,000 to purchase the artifacts. Nationwide newspapers,

This elk-hide shirt is a part of the Spalding-Allen Collection.

television, and radio stations asked people to give donations. The tribe contributed money. Schoolchildren held bake sales and car washes. Rock bands gave concerts. Two days before the deadline, children from an elementary school gave the tribe $2,500. It was the final amount needed for the Nez Perce to purchase their artifacts.

The artifacts can be seen at the Nez Perce National Historical Park Visitors' Center near Lapwai. At the visitors' center, the Nez Perce tell the story of the Ni mii pu, "the people."

Timeline

1700s	The Nez Perce acquire horses brought to the Americas by Spanish explorers in the 1500s.
1805	Lewis and Clark are helped by the Nez Perce on their journey to the Pacific Ocean.
1806	Lewis and Clark, returning eastward, are again helped by the Nez Perce.
1812	Fur trappers arrive in the Nez Perce homeland in search of beaver.
1831	Four Nez Perce travel to St. Louis, Missouri, to ask that someone be sent to teach the tribe about the Bible and to read and write.
1836	Henry and Eliza Spalding start a mission among the Nez Perce. Marcus and Narcissa Whitman start a mission among the Cayuse.
1841	Settlers begin traveling west along the Oregon Trail.
1847	A few Cayuse attack the Whitman Mission. U.S. soldiers come to avenge the attack. The Nez Perce stay out of the fighting.
1853	Washington becomes a United States territory. The Nez Perce sign a treaty with Territorial Governor Issac Stevens.
1856	Conflicts between settlers and several tribes lead to a war that lasts for two years. The Nez Perce do not fight against the soldiers.
1861	Thousands of miners come to Nez Perce lands in Idaho in search of gold.
1863	A new treaty reduces the Nez Perce lands to 757,000 acres (306,500 ha). The bands that do not sign the treaty become known as nontreaty bands.

continued next page

Timeline *continued*

1871	Old Joseph, leader of the nontreaty Wallowa band, dies. His son, Joseph, becomes the band's chief.
1877	The nontreaty bands are ordered to move to the lands retained in the 1863 treaty. The order results in a war that lasts five months as the bands try to escape to Canada. Chief Joseph surrenders to U.S. Army forces on October 5. Joseph and most of the survivors are sent to Kansas and later to Oklahoma.
1885	The survivors are allowed to return to Idaho from Oklahoma. However, Chief Joseph and his band are sent to Nespelem, Washington.
1887	Congress passes the General Allotment Act affecting all western tribes.
1892	Alice Fletcher completes the division of the Nez Perce's land.
1904	Chief Joseph dies.
1948	The Idaho Nez Perce sign their own constitution and become self-governing.
1965	The Nez Perce National Historical Park is established.
1999	The Nez Perce join with fifteen other American Indian tribes to help plan the National Lewis and Clark Bicentennial.

Glossary

ailment—a sickness

allotment—a parcel of land given to an individual

artifact—an object used by humans in the past

band—a group of people acting together for a common purpose

breed—to raise animals under controlled conditions

camas—a plant in the lily family

cradleboard—a leather pouch used to hold a baby

elder—an older person with experience and wisdom

emigrant—a person who moves from one place to live in another

ethnology—the study of people and their cultures

Great Plains—the prairie region of the United States

gristmill—a mill for grinding wheat into flour

kouse—a plant in the parsley family

missionary—a person sent by a church to teach religious beliefs

powwow—an important social gathering of American Indians

reed—a tall, slender grass that grows in wet or marshy places

reservation—land set aside for a special purpose

tepee—a cone-shaped tent made with poles and usually covered with animal skins

treaty—an agreement made in writing between two nations

tributary—a stream or river that flows into a larger stream or river

To Find Out More

Books

Bail, Raymond. *The Nez Perce.* New York: Benchmark Books, 2001.

Gaines, Richard M. *The Nez Perce.* Edina, Minnesota: Abdo & Daughters, 2001.

Lassieur, Allison. *The Nez Perce.* Mankato, Minnesota: Bridgestone Books, 2000.

McAuliffe, Bill and Lucile Davis. *Chief Joseph of the Nez Perce.* Mankato, Minnesota: Bridgestone Books, 1997.

Rifkin, Mark. *The Nez Perce Indians.* New York: Chelsea House Publishing, 1993.

Sneve, Virigina Driving Hawk. *The Nez Perce*. New York: Holiday House, 2001.

Taylor, Marian W. *Chief Joseph: Nez Perce Leader*. New York: Chelsea House Publishing, 1993.

Videos

Echoes of a Bitter Crossing. Modern-day explorers follow the Lewis and Clark trail over the Bitterroot Mountains, one of the most difficult parts of their journey. 60 minutes. (Idaho Public Television. www.idahoptv.org)

Sacred Journey of the Nez Perce. Remembrances of chiefs such as Joseph and White Bird presented by oral history stories, historical photos, and reenactment. 60 minutes. (Idaho Public Television. www.idahoptv.org)

Organizations and Online Sites

The Chief Joseph Foundation
P.O. Box 413
Lapwai, Idaho 83540
http://www.scenic-idaho.com/chiefjosephfoundation
This foundation promotes Nez Perce cultural preservation and is centered around Appaloosa horses that are descendants of Ollokot's Appaloosas.

Confederated Tribes of the Colville Indian Reservation
P.O. Box 150
Nespelem, Washington 99155
http://www.colvilletribes.com
This is the official site for the Colville Tribes, which has information about their government, history, and tribal events.

Confederated Tribes of the Umatilla Indian Reservation
P.O. Box 638
Pendleton, Oregon 97801
http://www.umatilla.nsn.us
This site provides historical and present-day information about the Cayuse, Umatilla, and Walla Walla tribes. It also shows the text of their 1855 treaty with the United States Government.

National Park Service
U.S. Department of the Interior
Washington, D.C.
http://www.nps.gov
The National Park Service oversees hundreds of parks and historic places in the United States, including locations important in Nez Perce history. This site presents information about the Nez Perce National Historical Park and Big Hole National Battlefield.

Nez Perce Tribe
P.O. Box 365
Lapwai, Idaho 83540
http://www.nezperce.org
This is the official site of the Nez Perce Tribe. It has information about the tribal council and the business they conduct for tribal members, including health and human resources, forestry, fisheries, education, and law enforcement. It also presents historical facts about the Nez Perce.

University of Washington Libraries Digital Collections
http://content.lib.washington.edu/aipnw/walker/
This site presents historical essays about the Nez Perce.

A Note on Sources

We first became interested in the Nez Perce while writing the book *Cruising the Columbia and Snake Rivers*. We read the journals of Lewis and Clark and learned how important the Nez Perce were to the explorers' success. With the journals in hand, we traveled by tugboat and sailboat along the 1805 route Lewis and Clark followed to the Pacific Ocean. They rode in canoes the Nez Perce had helped them make.

To begin writing this book, we reread the Lewis and Clark journals and traveled to Washington, D.C., to study material in the Library of Congress. Then we visited the archives of state historical societies in Idaho, Oregon, and Washington; our local libraries; and university web sites. Because the Nez Perce were so important to the opening of the west, we found many sources for research.

With our search of the literature nearly complete, we began our fieldwork. We traveled to Oregon's Wallowa Valley for the annual Chief Joseph Days celebration. At a Nez Perce Friendship Feast, we talked with Soy Redthunder, a great-grandson of Chief Joseph, and Horace Axtell, whose book, *A Little Bit of Wisdom*, provided valuable information.

The next day we drove to Spalding, Idaho, along the route of an ancient Nez Perce trail. From the highway, we looked down into a deep canyon where Old Joseph's band spent each winter. At Spalding at the headquarters of the Nez Perce National Historical Park, Robert Applegate, the park's archivist, and Diane Mallickan, the park's cultural interpreter, assisted us. Diane, a Nez Perce, speaks the Nez Perce language, which she learned from her grandparents.

On a second trip, we visited with Vera Sonneck, Director of the Cultural Resource Program at the Nez Perce Tribal Headquarters in Lapwai, Idaho. Then we continued along highways in Idaho and Montana that parallel the steep trails used by the Nez Perce on their way to hunt buffalo and visited many of the 1877 battlefields.

Having gathered facts, stories, and feelings for where the Nez Perce roamed and now live, we wrote this book.

—Sharlene and Ted Nelson

Index

Numbers in *italics* indicate illustrations.

About the Authors

Sharlene and Ted Nelson were married after their graduation from the University of California at Berkeley. As Ted began his forestry career, the couple lived in a remote logging camp in northern California. While living there, Sharlene began freelance writing and raising their two children. Later, the couple moved to Washington, North Carolina, and Oregon. At each location, they pursued their interest in history.

They have written guidebooks to the Columbia and Snake Rivers and West Coast lighthouses. For their first book for Franklin Watts, they wrote about logging in the Old West. Their Children's Press books have been about national parks and monuments, the Golden Gate Bridge, and a biography. The Nelsons appeared in the PBS series *Legendary Lighthouses*.

Their home in Washington overlooks the waters of Puget Sound and the Olympic Mountains. When not researching and writing, they ski, hike, and sail.